your heart
will heal

a gentle guided journal
for getting over anyone

chrissy
stockton

THOUGHT
CATALOG
Books

THOUGHTCATALOG.COM
NEW YORK · LOS ANGELES

THOUGHT
CATALOG
Books

Published by Thought Catalog Books, an imprint of the digital magazine Thought Catalog, which is owned and operated by The Thought & Expression Company LLC, an independent media organization based in Brooklyn, New York and Los Angeles, California.

This book was produced by Chris Lavergne and Noelle Beams. Art direction and design by KJ Parish. Special thanks to Chrissy Stockton for creative editorial direction and Isidoros Karamitopoulos for circulation management.

Visit us on the web at thoughtcatalog.com and shopcatalog.com.

Made in the USA.

ISBN 9781949759150

the breakup

There are few things we encounter in our lives so startling and disorienting as a breakup. One day you're walking down the street and everything makes sense. An hour later, your world is upended and it seems like everyone else is speaking a foreign language. Even listening to it hits a strange note in your ear.

You loved someone, and now they are gone.

You find yourself left with the unenviable task of learning how to stop loving someone you don't want to stop loving. You have to let someone go before you are ready. Since we are rational animals, doing something before you've convinced yourself it needs to be done is a difficult task! That's why this journal is here for you. It can push you forward each day so that you get a little bit closer to being able to move on.

The exercises in this journal are geared toward experiencing the whole spectrum of fun emotions you feel during a breakup: shock, denial, grief, sadness, insecurity, and anger. They are meant to make you feel supported through your pain, like a trusted friend who knows how much it sucks but also knows that it will get better. You can skip around, or you can commit to doing one journal entry each day in order. If one chapter really speaks to you, you can even use that as a weekly entry and keep updating your journal on the same topic. If the pages of this book seem too small or confining in any way, grab a notebook to keep journaling as you read. If you aren't inspired to write, find some colored markers and doodle until you're ready. Writing your way through these exercises will help get your feelings out of your head. It's one way to make sure you are processing your emotions and taking concrete steps to move on.

If it feels like you're drowning in an excess of negative feelings, this journal should help you to know you have something concrete to do each day. You have a way to move forward.

This guided journal will help you address all the aspects of your breakup. It will cover subjects more than once to help you see what's going on from different perspectives. If a chapter isn't working for you, move on to the next one. If you feel bored by the topic, choose another one. When you feel you've moved on and no longer need the support to work through a subject, don't feel like you need to complete it just to have something written down. There are other pages that might be calling out to you if you leave your mind open and page through this book. Let your intuition guide you; there is no right or wrong way to use this journal.

My hope is that when you use this journal, you feel at peace. I hope that every day you can see a little more clearly how you are going to survive your breakup. There's a whole life ahead of you that should be made more and more appealing each time you use this journal to get perspective.

it's okay to feel bad : (

A teaching in Buddhism is about the second arrow. The idea is that sometimes in life we are injured (being hit by an arrow), and that is unavoidable. We make matters worse by allowing ourselves to be hit with a second arrow. The first arrow is the bad thing that happens to us; the second arrow is our response to it.

Often, what we do to avoid feeling pain becomes the thing which actually causes us the most pain.

If you sit with your pain and feel it, you will discover it isn't that bad; it is something you can manage. What causes you more pain is the second arrow: worrying about if you will feel pain again tomorrow, or worrying that you are somehow broken for experiencing the pain in the first place, or wondering if it's normal to feel so *much* and if everyone else is experiencing the world in a different (and better) way. We don't have enough control in life to avoid ever being hurt (the first arrow), but we do control the way we respond to being hurt. We control the second arrow.

Your only job today is to let yourself feel your pain. The longer you avoid feeling your pain, the longer you will be in pain. Climb into bed and set an alarm for 5 minutes. Let your mind wander to different parts of your body; what do you notice? What does your loss feel like?

Some people feel a tightness in their chest. They realize they are tensing their shoulders up toward their ears. Some people will realize their breathing is shallow. Pay attention to what you are feeling and allow yourself to truly *feel* it. This is how you will let it go.

Journal: List the ways you are hurting. Document as many painful thoughts as you can, even if they seem small or silly—get them out on paper. Notice what surprising thoughts come to mind. You can feel confident that every one of these thoughts is going to fade with time. In just 24 hours when you come back to your journal, you will already feel some space from these thoughts.

- I am hurting b/c I know what could've been
- I'm hurting b/c I'll miss our dog
- I'm hurting b/c I had to leave.
- I'm hurting b/c he was clueless
- I'm hurting b/c I stayed for so long

- I'm hurting b/c I'd rather not be
- I'm hurting b/c I felt like my only option was to leave.
- I'm hurting b/c it hurts.
- I'm hurting b/c I can't numb myself anymore.
- I'm hurting b/c I had to let go of him, even though I loved him.
- I'm hurting b/c he still didn't get it.
- I'm hurting b/c I loved him. I feel it less now.

move the body & the mind follows

Today you are going to do some tough work. Today you are going to take action toward curating the life that you want. Today you are going to scrub your skin and emerge with pink cheeks: raw and sensitive to the world and new and ready to be touched.

What will your life look like when you have moved on from this relationship? Take time today to physically make your life look more like what you envision with the faith that "if you build it, they will come." Make sure your home is free from any items belonging to your ex. Enlist a friend if something needs to be returned to them. Remove photos of your ex from anywhere you would immediately see them, such as any displayed in your home or immediately visible on your phone, computer, or social media accounts.

You don't have to completely remove your ex from your life; you just have to remove them from what is immediately visible or accessible. Mute, unfollow, block, or unfriend on social media—whatever you need to do so that they don't pop up unannounced. If you will be tempted to post on social media performatively (with the hope that they will view and respond to your post), consider what actions you can take to remove this impulse.

Removing someone physically (and digitally) from your life might seem extreme or impossible, but it will create the space you need to heal and move on. Let all the business you have with your ex be finished. You can even use this phrase as a mantra when they pop into your thoughts:

$$\left(\begin{array}{l}\text{"All the business I have} \\ \text{with my ex is finished."}\end{array}\right)$$

Going through the motions of something being true is the step you take right before that thing actually becomes true. Act like you believe for as many days as you need to, and one day you will wake up and it won't be an act. Your job today is to close out a chapter so that you can begin to anticipate turning the page to a new one.

Journal: List ways that your ex may still be "stuck" in your life, and brainstorm how you can eliminate or best deal with each way.

- I've blocked him and his friends from social media, deleted all photos, and removed all his gifts from my life.
- He's still a co-signer for a loan, but I can refinance as soon as I'm done (w/grad school).

- I can't remove my memories, but I can avoid his neighborhood.

how you feel today is not how you will feel forever

There is no perpetual motion machine. The emotions you feel about this breakup are finite; there is an end to them. It is not possible that you will feel the intensity of emotions you feel today forever. Like a wave, your negative feelings will reach a crest and then cascade forward and flatten out. It won't happen today, but you can feel secure knowing that it is absolutely inevitable that your suffering will come to an end.

Nothing is permanent.

Spend a few minutes thinking back to some times in your life when you have felt particularly upset, low, grieving, or anxious. Those feelings didn't last forever. You're not feeling them with the same intensity today. In fact, you can probably pick out some positive things that happened as a result of the events that cause you to feel badly. It may be crystal clear now to see why a previous breakup was in your best interests or why the end of a difficult job has brought you to a better place professionally.

We tend to experience life in cycles of events that challenge us: We meet an obstacle and are challenged by it, work on overcoming it, and then experience a period of happiness or relief while we enjoy having had some conclusion and respite from the challenge. No matter where we are in life, we never stay in one phase of this cycle for too long. Just as happiness doesn't last forever, neither does sadness.

Your only job today is to allow yourself the comfort of knowing that you will not feel this way forever.

Journal: Make a list of things from your past that were very difficult at the time and think about whether you would truly go back and avoid that pain if you could. What positive experiences have you had in your life because of what you have gone through?

• When I was 16, I didn't get Maria in west side story. Looking back, I know I wasn't prepared for that kind of role, and it challenged me to be a better performer.

• I didn't get into some colleges for my undergrad. I'm glad b/c wcc has taught me so much, and I've made lasting connections and memories there.

- I recently didn't get cast as Alspina. I was very upset b/c I felt like my hard work was not acknowledged, but now I know it's b/c of my lack as a singer. I've learned more about myself as a singer since then, and know which roles to aim for.

willingness

Today you are going to be willing to imagine that a future without your ex is happier and healthier and more *full* than the past you had with them. You do not have to believe this is true (that will take time); you just have to be willing to consider that it *might* be true.

Everyone has stories they tell themselves in a relationship about why this one is The One.

Maybe you and your ex had a particularly cute meeting that sounds like something an old couple would tell their great-grandchildren after their 60th wedding anniversary and everyone would remember them for what a Great Love they had. Or maybe your ex is the only person you've ever met who loves Van Morrison as much as you do. Or they want to travel to all the same places, and everyone else you meet is some kind of a homebody. Or your parents love them. Or their last name sounds really good with your first name.

These aren't real reasons to end up with someone, but they are the things we tell ourselves. We think they are little signs from the universe that this romance was meant to be for now and forever. Let it go. You will have a version of these things with the next person and the one after that. *When you meet the right person, you won't need to string together little cute stories to tell people why you love each other.*

All you have to do today is acknowledge that maybe this story about your relationship isn't the only (or best!) story about a relationship you will ever have.

I thought our mutual connection to WCC meant that this was meant to be. We both had a shared passion for music; we had good times hanging out.

He would come to my shows; he would give me flowers and gifts.

His gestures seemed sincere.

I guess his sincerity was fake.

I guess all of it

was just a pretense of
what love-owns-like.
I deserve more
than just a show or
a pretense. I deserve
deep, true love. Not
just a show.

you are enough

While you worry about the ways you weren't appreciated by your ex, it's easy to forget about all the things you bring to the table. Whether they valued your assets or not, you have them. Every person on the planet has good things about them, and there are people who appreciate these things. Because you are so familiar with your particular good attributes, you don't notice them, or you make excuses about how they aren't that great or as good as what someone else has to offer. Your practice today is to begin to list the good things so that you can start to shift your perspective and see yourself the way another partner might.

Whether or not your ex noticed the good things about you says more about their particular values and ability to notice and appreciate the good in other people than it does about whether *you* are good or worthy.

Journal: Write down nice things you can remember people saying to you or about you. Write as many as you can remember, even if they seem small, even if they come from people who "have" to love you like your parents. You can go through some old emails or cards to help jog your memory. Maybe you will just list qualities you *think* people appreciate about you. The important thing is to spend some time today trying to see yourself through the eyes of people who love you.

- People say I have a lovely voice
- that I've grown a lot as a musician.
- That I've grown a lot as a person
- that I'm reliable
- that I'm honest
- that I'm determined
- that I'm funny
- that I'm creative
- that I'm responsible
- that I'm thoughtful
- that I'm "type A"

no, seriously, you are enough

There is no reason to assume that you being single has anything to do with not being "enough," because we can look around and see that people on all ends of every kind of spectrum have found love. Love does not just happen to beautiful, perfect, thin, intelligent, happy, successful, or rich people. For every bad quality you worry about possessing, there is someone in the world with that quality in abundance who has found love.

Journal: Talk about your big fears. Even if it's not rational, what worries you about the end of your relationship? What insecurities are presenting themselves? Next, think about other people with those same attributes—are they all single and miserable? Of course not!

- I'm worried no one will want me
- I'm worried I'll be alone forever
- I'm worried that I won't heal.

- I'm worried I'm terrible in relationships
- I'm worried no one finds me pretty
- I'm worried it's too soon to fall over him.
- I'm worried that I won't ever heal from that relation-ship
- I'm worried it's too soon to be okay.
- I'm worried I'm worried.
- I'm worried that I'm not a good partner.

say it with me: your worth is not up for debate

Your soul is not insufficient. You may have learned that someone doesn't love you the way you wish they would, but you also learned that you have the ability to love. You learned all the things you are capable of doing when it comes to caring for another human being.

Think about all the things you did in your relationship, all the ways you loved someone so well. They don't get to take this away from you. You own all the ways you are able to be healthy and give love to someone.

Maybe this person was unable to see or appreciate the ways you loved them, but that doesn't mean you didn't do a good job of it. For today, focus on your abilities as a partner, on the things someone else will be able to recognize.

Journal: Make a list of the ways you did a good job of loving someone. Think about how lucky it would feel to have a partner as good at loving someone as you are.

- I was consistent
- I tried to do them favors
- I tried to cater to their needs
- I listened to them
- I tried to plan fun things for them.
- I tried to be there for them.
- I was reliable
- I comforted them.
- I tried to make them happy.

"What did I do wrong?"

Breakups are only rarely about you doing something wrong, though it is impossible to go through a breakup and not think, "What did I do wrong?" about a hundred times a day.

The most likely reason you broke up is simply that you weren't right for each other. It's a question of fit and balance and meeting the right person at the right time—not of being good enough or never making a mistake. Even if you did fuck up, it happens! Now you know how to love the next person better.

None of this means that you are unlovable or that you won't find someone who loves you in the future.

The important thing is that your mistakes in this relationship, whether real or imagined, are no longer relevant or worth punishing yourself for. You can't make someone stick with you through good behavior. That's not an enviable relationship. Repeat this Dita von Teese quote to yourself as often as you need to: *"You can be the ripest, juiciest peach in the world, and there's still going to be somebody who hates peaches."* All you can do is your best, and one day that will be more than enough for someone.

Journal: Make a list of things you did "wrong" in your relationship. Take time to read over the list and notice how it feels in your rational mind. You will be able to easily tell these are your insecurities talking, not a good argument made by truly rational thinking.

it's okay to cry

It doesn't make you weak to cry.

It doesn't make you stupid to feel emotions.

Your ex has a vested stake in making you feel bad about feeling bad. They may try to gaslight you by pointing out you "weren't serious" or some variation of that. It helps them to feel as if they don't need to be guilty because your pain isn't their responsibility. Unfortunately, both can be true.

Maybe your ex did everything on the up and up and tried their best to make you feel good, and it still didn't work out. That's okay, too. That doesn't mean you're wrong for feeling rejected, angry, sad, or broken. Whatever you feel is the correct thing to feel.

Today, all you have to do is not punish yourself for feeling what you feel.

Journal: Write about your feelings and notice whenever you try to shift your thoughts away from something. What feelings are you trying not to feel?

the next bus leaves in five minutes

Strategist and writer Stephanie St. Clair says it best. When it comes to relationships, "The next bus leaves in five minutes."

This was not your one and only shot at love.

The story of your life is not built around this one relationship that ended. The story of your life is a series of challenges and the way you resolve them. Every day is full of opportunities and second chances. There will be no shortage of ways for you to move on when you are ready.

We are tempted to have a scarcity mindset where we grieve each lost opportunity as if another will never come along. But we know from experience that the story never ends. There is no "happily ever after," but there is also no point at which something so bad has happened to us that we are stuck there and nothing good will happen again. Everything—good or bad—comes to an end and is replaced by something else. When we grieve the end of one relationship, we can also feel confident that one day—after we have become capable of letting go of the past—we will have the opportunity to start again.

Your job today is to tell yourself that "the next bus leaves in five minutes." You are not stuck here forever grieving this relationship.

One day you will be excited and able to see the opportunities all around you.

Journal: Write down a few things you are excited for now that you couldn't be excited for while you were in your relationship. Even while you are immersed in the pain of breaking up, there are things that will emerge as positives, no matter how small. Hold on to them.

social media detox

During this period it is SO tempting to stalk your ex. You will want to see what they are tweeting or where they are going on Instagram. It's very natural, but it's also making it impossible for you to let go. It's also adding pain to your daily routine.

Here's where you can enlist a friend to help you. Outsource the task of stalking your ex to a close friend who knows you well. This way, you can be confident that you will know anything you need to know, but you can get yourself out of the habit of obsessively following them around the internet. Block/unfriend/mute them so that you know you won't stumble across them unintentionally.

You and your friend can have a conversation about how much information you want them to give you about what your ex is doing, and you can aim to gradually decrease the amount of information you crave. Whether they give you a daily briefing text or your friend vows to tell you only if it seems like they're dating someone new (or some other milestone you want to be aware of), this is one way you can give yourself distance from the relationship and create the space you need to move on.

Journal: Write down what you're afraid you'll "miss" if you don't stalk your ex on social media. Use this list to guide your conversation with your friend.

welcome to the wide world of breakup music

The best part of breaking up is being able to listen to an entire world of breakup music and feel it vibrate from your heart and your bones and know it was written just for you. Breakup songs are the best kind of music. They help you realize that you are far from alone—that every beautiful, talented, intelligent, creative genius has felt what you are feeling at one point in time. They are writing these hits for you.

Enjoy one of the few perks of breaking up and discover (or re-discover) music that could have been written by your very own sub-conscious. Make a playlist of songs that speak to you and listen to it while you walk or drive alone. It's crazy how many emotions you can process through a long walk with Taylor Swift's *1989* playing in your headphones. And the goal IS to process emotions, not to run from them. Spending time feeling all your breakup feelings is how you are going to be able to let them go and leave them in the past.

Journal: List breakup songs that will go on your playlist. Write out the line from each song that speaks to the way you feel right now. Make your playlist. Listen to it regularly.

beware of bread crumbs

You will want to reach out to your ex. You will want to tell them something serious like how much you miss them or something silly like a joke that you found that you know they'd enjoy. This is normal; they were a part of your life. They were a person you shared things with; it will take a while to undo this.

They might even reach out to you for this same reason. But you cannot allow yourself to be happy with bread crumbs.

Bread crumbs are morsels of attention someone gives you to keep you interested in them because they like the feeling of having you on their hook—not because they are actually interested in having a relationship with you. A bread crumb feels like hope. It feels like your ex is minutes away from telling you what an idiot they were, that the whole breakup was a mistake. But if they really felt that way, they'd give you more than a morsel. If they loved you and were ready to take you back, they'd give you more than a morsel. They would speak their mind intentionally and honestly. Anything less is a game, and it's not fair to you.

Journal: Write down any "morsels" you want to send your ex. Talk about how these make you feel and what they say about your personality. If you loved how you and your ex had the same sense of humor, reflect on how that is something you want to look for in the future. If you want to send them something nice, think about what a loving, nurturing person you are and how lucky your next love is. Through this process, you'll be able to grieve for the loss of a friend and reflect on what's important to you in relationships and how you would like to be seen by your beloved.

it's none of your business how your ex is doing

It's none of your business if they miss you.

It's none of your business if they need you.

It's none of your business if they still love you.

It's not your responsibility to make sure your ex is getting through this breakup or that they have their questions answered or that knowing they hurt you isn't too much of a burden for them to bear. You will know how someone feels about you by their actions, not their words. At the very end of the day, your ex *showed* you how much they valued you, and it's not enough. They are no longer your responsibility.

It's also not your responsibility to dispense justice at them. If they wronged you, they have to live with themselves being someone who lies to the person they love, or cheats on them, or whatever else. You get to move on and leave them in the past, which is definitely the preferable position to be in.

Your responsibility is to serve your own best interest, which is to be able to process emotion until you feel neutrally about your ex so that you can move on and be happy. Indulging in romantic or revenge fantasies is going to continue to fuel the wrong kind of feelings. The sooner you can let go, the sooner you can move on.

Journal: Most people during a breakup focus on wanting their ex back. Your goal today is to convince yourself that your life really will be better once you can let go of all feelings toward your ex. Write about what your life will look like when all your longing or anger is in the past.

"Why is it so easy for everyone else?"

One of the ways we punish ourselves after a breakup is to look around and see how "easy" relationships seem to be for everyone else. This is only true because we typically see the happy moments in people's lives from the outside; we're given less information about their struggles or what it costs for them to have those happy moments. There aren't many glamorous "I got ghosted" photos on Instagram.

In truth, you know a lot of relationships are not as happy as they appear. Think carefully about the relationships where you are privy to behind-the-scenes information. Would you be willing to deal with the downsides of that relationship for you personally? Would you accept someone who makes risky decisions with money in order to have the benefit of a sharp dresser? Could you deal with someone very opinionated about political issues? Would you really love being with someone who was obsessed with fitness, or would you resent the time they spent at the gym and having to accommodate someone else's strict diet? Or maybe you are the one into fitness and you wouldn't match well with someone who wouldn't support or join you in this arena. The point isn't that everyone is secretly unhappy; it's that other people's relationships are never as aspirational as they seem.

In relationships, no one has it easy. We are all imperfect humans dealing with other imperfect humans. Our job is to find someone who is a good partner who complements our individual strengths and weaknesses, and vice versa. Every relationship is hard, and the point is to find the hard that feels right for us instead of comparing ourselves to other people and what they have chosen for themselves.

Journal: Write down all of your ex's pros and cons. Feel a sense of relief as you realize you are not tying yourself down to a lifetime of living with someone who has these flaws. Think about if you've learned anything about your needs and deal-breakers because of this relationship. Additionally, now that you've been on an oxytocin break from your ex, you may notice that the items in the "pros" column don't seem as big, rare, and unattainable as they did before.

you do not have to process your breakup perfectly

Love is not rational, so you should not punish yourself for being irrational about love. The part of our brain that makes us feel "in love" is the same part of our brain that causes someone to be addicted to cocaine or keep gambling long after they've lost it all. Letting go of someone and moving on after a relationship is difficult and involves undoing attachments and emotions that don't change overnight.

Do not make yourself feel bad that loving someone is not a switch you can just turn off. This is not weakness. This is the physiological reality of how it works for everyone, as long as they're not a sociopath.

Today, consider whether you have any guilt about how quickly or perfectly you are processing your breakup. Remind yourself that it is normal and healthy to "still" feel badly about the breakup or have feelings for your ex. It's also the time to forgive and be gentle with yourself about any embarrassing things you've done in this breakup. If you've sent a desperate text or driven by their house just to see their face, you're not the first or last person in the world to make a mistake because you thought at the time it would make your heart feel better.

Journal: Think about the stress you are placing on yourself to grieve your breakup in a certain way. What feelings are you trying not to feel?

the way to "win" the breakup is to not care about winning the breakup

It's tempting to throw all of our energy into "winning" a breakup. It gives us something to do, a list to check off—it makes us feel in control. We think we can show someone what they were missing, the extent of the mistake they made, and then we will finally feel better.

When you are putting energy into winning a breakup, you are putting energy into the breakup instead of releasing energy from the breakup.

You will stay stuck in your feelings for/about the other person much longer if you are feeding your revenge fantasy. It's okay to feel the impulse to post a picture specifically to show your ex how good/happy you look, but you can recognize this feeling is unhelpful and choose to focus on what will help you get to the next stage instead of what will make it look as if you are already there.

You win a breakup by moving on. You win by having neutral feelings about your ex instead of sad or angry or loving feelings—and when you have these neutral feelings, you stop caring about "winning" to begin with.

Journal: Make a list of all the fantasy ways you could "win" the breakup and get it out of your system. Focus on the strong feelings you feel when you think about winning your ex's approval or getting "even" with them. Think about how attached to your ex you still feel when you think about doing these things. When you're ready, make a new list of things that would make you happy right now that have nothing to do with your ex. Do one of those things.

reach out to friends

When you break up with someone, you lose the social life you had built with them. It's important to be intentional in filling in the time you used to spend with your ex with other people. You may feel the impulse to be a homebody and do nothing but stay at home with Netflix and pizza, but you really will feel better when you spend time with other people. Schedule dates with friends, text people you've lost touch with, throw a dinner party, or plan a trip out of town for a weekend.

Make a habit of saying "yes" to social invitations you get.

You might not feel like you're ready to be in the "wearing less and going out more" phase of your breakup, but this is a fake-it-until-you-make-it kind of thing. You *will* feel better by having more social contact. You will rediscover parts of you that you'd forgotten—because they didn't fit the person your ex wanted you to be. You will regain confidence in your social skills and that you are perfectly adept at relationships and desirable as a companion, regardless of how it worked out with this one person.

Journal: Think about your life before your relationship. What people made you feel good when you spent time with them? Make a list, make a plan, and reach out.

sleep in the middle of the bed

When you live life with another person, you make a series of adjustments so that you work better together. You sleep on a certain side of the bed, make habits that account for going to sleep/waking up at the same time, or do things like watch television with the volume down and the lights on because that's how they enjoy it, when you're really a lights-off-and-volume-up kind of person. There are a lot of little ways we all slowly develop a "relationship personality" that we have the freedom to unlearn after a breakup.

The fun part is that now you get to be selfish. You don't have to compromise for anyone.

Sleep in the middle of the bed. Make whatever kind of weird food you most enjoy, and eat it standing up over the sink or surrounded by fancy candles if that's what you want. Keep your home as clean or as messy as you want, and know that the only person who is dirtying it is you. Get a cat if your ex was allergic to them. Follow the little impulses you only get to follow when you are the only person in your life you need to please.

You might discover something that you never want to have to give up again. Maybe you realized that your ex made you bend too much, that you were trying harder to please them than seems fair in what's supposed to be a partnership. Give yourself room to explore your wants and needs free from outside influence. Take note of what you want to hold onto most in your next relationship.

Journal: What compromises did you make for your ex? Who do you want to be now?

Flowers can't always be blooming

You are not expected to be happy all the time. The story of life is that it moves in cycles and seasons. Sometimes the purpose of your life is to be planting seeds, and sometimes it's to be enjoying the harvest. As bad as it feels right now, it is only one season and every winter turns into spring at some point.

Know that your only job right now is to weather the storm. A storm that *will* end. One day you will wake up and your first thought won't be of your ex. One day you will wake up and be ready to meet someone new. One day you will go an entire day without wondering what they are doing. Trust that this cyclical nature is at play and that you just need to put one foot in front of the other until you look up and realize the landscape has changed.

Journal: Write about other times in your life where things have seemed bad and even like they may never get better. Remember that those, too, were only seasons. They come and go.

Smudge

Sage is a plant that can be burned in order to cleanse energy. This may not be part of your religious or cultural history, but the placebo effect can be helpful here. If you spend part of one evening burning sage in your home and thinking about how you are ready to let go of the energy from your past relationship and invite in new energy, it will be beneficial even if there are no actual mysterious, metaphysical benefits at play.

You can buy a 3-pack on Amazon for $8. Light one (keep it on a candle tray or something that won't burn/melt) and wander around your house making sure that you get the smoke everywhere. Pay special attention to hitting the four corners of every doorway. Think about how you are "cleaning" the energy of your home. You are saying goodbye. You are saying hello. You are ready to wake up tomorrow and have your fresh start.

Journal: List three things you want to let go of and three things you want to invite into your life. Walk around your space burning sage and thinking about letting go and inviting in these things.

understand what you are leaving behind

It's the easiest thing in the world to romanticize a relationship after it's over. If you were dumped you can probably fill a novel with the questions you've asked yourself about why you "weren't good enough." You focus on the things you miss and sometimes you even completely forget about the ways you were unhappy in your relationship.

Some people slowly realize what they are feeling after a breakup isn't a loss of the person they broke up with, but a reaction to being rejected.

It's important to differentiate between normal feelings of insecurity after a rejection and actually grieving the loss of someone from your life. *Do you really miss them, or are your feelings just hurt?* When you demystify the things you are sad to have lost, you can have more perspective about how big or small that loss actually is.

Journal: Make a long list of little things that weren't right in your relationship. Are you missing a romanticized version of your ex? Were there any ways you felt like you couldn't completely be yourself? Use today to try to get more perspective about what specifically you are having strong feelings about missing when you think about the breakup.

let go of the banana

Author Ronit Baras wrote a story about how easy it is to trap a big monkey in a small cage: "You place a banana inside the cage and leave an opening large enough for the monkey's hand, but not for the banana. As soon as the monkey grabs the banana, it's trapped. The monkey can set itself free if it lets go of the banana, but it won't! By not giving up what it has in its hand, it locks itself just outside the tiny cage."

You are free to go wherever you want as soon as you learn to let go. Most people want to move on but tell themselves they can't for X reason. You think your ex is the only person in the world who won't be turned off by your crooked teeth or the shape of your belly. You tell yourself that what you had was irreplaceably special because you have the same favorite musical artist.

There are other bananas in the world.

There are other fruits to enjoy.

This is not the last banana you will ever encounter.

Let go of the banana.

Journal: Write about what thoughts, habits, or beliefs are you holding onto at the expense of not being able to move forward.

why you haven't been able to "brush it off"

It sucks to feel rejected, whether the rejection is someone ghosting you after two weeks or breaking your heart after two years or even making you dump them because they rejected you by not investing their energy into the relationship.

Unfortunately, knowing rejection sucks for everyone doesn't make it hurt any less.

Just remember that it doesn't make you crazy or overly emotional to not be able to brush a relationship off. Not everything is meant to be brushed off. One of the things we as humans need to survive is the companionship of others. We are not a species made to be vulnerable and intimate with someone one moment and feel completely emotionless about them the next.

Feeling attached to someone is the price of admission for being close to anyone. Sometimes you get hurt and the hurt sticks around for a little while. It's okay. It will pass. You will wake up better, stronger, and more resilient one day. Be patient and be grateful for your humanity.

Journal: Make a list of things you are able to do well because you are able to feel the full range of human emotion. For instance, are you a loving dog owner? A loyal friend? Do you give great advice because of your ability to empathize? Today is about understanding that your humanity is a gift.

a few reminders that what you are feeling is temporary

"You can't connect the dots looking forward; you can only connect them looking backward. So you have to trust that the dots will somehow connect in your future. You have to trust in something—your gut, destiny, life, karma, whatever. This approach has never let me down, and it has made all the difference in my life." —Steve Jobs

"Hold on to the thought that no emotion lasts forever, no matter how wonderful or how terrible the emotion may be. The tears may last a little longer than you would like, but it will get better. I promise." —Osayi Osar-Emokpae

"Life always waits for some crisis to occur before revealing itself at its most brilliant." —Paulo Coelho

"The harder you slam a ball into the ground, the higher it bounces back up....A divorce, a breakup, losing a job, or just feeling seriously down can ground you, rough you up a bit, leave calluses on your feet and grit under your fingernails. But more than that, it leaves you wiser and stronger next time." —Laurel House

"If it weren't for hitting 'rock bottom' I never would have had this amazing hill of life to climb back up." —Peter Kraus

"Without Voldemort, Harry Potter is a very ordinary boy." —Elizabeth Gilbert

"Sometimes you need to scorch everything to the ground and start over. After the burning the soil is richer, and new things can grow. People are like that, too. They start over. They find a way." —Celeste Ng

Journal: Write about one of these quotes that genuinely made you feel better and what was helpful about it for you to remember.

what to do when you're stuck on your ex being "perfect" for you

No one is perfect for anyone else, but when you are leaving a relationship you can get stuck thinking about all the ways your ex is irreplaceable. You spent a lot of time in your head building up your future with them. You dreamed of the life you thought you were going to have together. And some people actually *are* great. Sometimes you're in a relationship with someone who truly makes you better or exposes you to the kind of world you want to live in.

But they aren't the only person who can do that.

You already know this is true if you think back to your earlier relationships or crushes and the way you were convinced so many people were your ticket to this life you wanted at that time. But you let go of them and your life went on. You forged your own way.

Journal: Everything feels more doable when you can name it. Write about the life you thought you were going to have with your ex. Be as specific as possible. You don't have to let go of this life and these dreams today. Just be willing to let go of the idea that your ex is the only person who could take this journey with you.

what gift is your breakup going to give you?

The first noble truth of Buddhism is that life is permeated by suffering. This life isn't *supposed* to be heaven, and we're not here for a tea party. Our purpose is to take our suffering on the chin and try to learn from it and become good and wise people. This can be a gift.

If you think about it now, I bet you can consider how each of your past breakups was actually a blessing. Your life went onward and upward from that person.

This breakup is a challenge, and you can use it as an opportunity to learn how to love and heal yourself. Your ex may have provided you with some valuable information about your faults as a partner. Or you may have discovered that you are quicker to anger than you would like to be or that you would rather be unhappy in a relationship than risk being single. (A warning: Make sure to run your thoughts by a trusted friend and ask for feedback—just because your ex said you were bad at something or made you feel bad about something doesn't mean you actually *were* bad. You'll need to separate out someone being bitter or abusive from someone making a genuine criticism about your personality.)

Use this time to learn about yourself as a partner and lover and make some authentic effort to improve.

Journal: Write about something you would like to take this time to focus on and improve. Include at least one action step like ordering a book about how to be healthy when you deal with conflict, or download a meditation app if your goal is to have a longer fuse.

quit the fantasy

It's tempting to salve the hurt of a breakup by numbing out with a nice juicy daydream about how great the happy moments with your ex were. Zoning out and remembering the good times can take up a lot of time in the day when you'd prefer not to spend thinking about other things, like how they don't love you anymore and whether you're ever going to find love again. But each fantasy prolongs the life of the relationship in your head. The goal isn't to hold on; the goal is to let go.

A psychic once told me that if you are having thoughts you don't want to have, like thinking about someone who probably isn't thinking about you, you can imagine "crossing out" the thought with your fingers or pressing the cancel button in your brain. You have to stop actively indulging in thoughts about your ex in whatever method works for you.

Journal: Brainstorm a few ways you are going to try to stop thinking about your ex. Dream up a new fantasy you're going to think about before you fall asleep where your favorite movie star shows up at your door to do research for their next role. Think about a "crossing out" technique that feels made for you. If you're a reader, maybe each time you think about your ex you will visualize turning the page of your thoughts to a new, blank sheet. If you like art, think about painting over thoughts of your ex with thick strokes of heavy paint. You can even take this exercise into the real world and head to a beach and write your ex's name in the sand to watch the waves wash it away or write it in chalk somewhere you can erase it with water.

get it all out

The first step of healing is figuring out what you're supposed to be healing from.

You need to get all of our feelings for your ex out on paper so that you can examine them and move forward.

You need to understand how your ex has hurt you.

This is like ripping the Band-Aid off; it might hurt before it gets better, but by the time you get to the end you're going to feel more space between you and the person you are trying to move on from.

Journal: Write a letter to your ex. Settle in—it's going to be a long letter. Include every way they've hurt you. Ask them all the questions you still have. Tell them exactly why you think they're a jerk and what they could have done better. Include every little thought that's lingering in your mind. Leave it all on the page. **[Use separate paper for this one.]**

thinking about missing them is worse than actually missing them

Getting over someone is a waiting game. After a certain amount of time, you will get over them. You won't even be able to help it. Time makes every loss more manageable.

The worst part of breaking up with someone is thinking that it is always going to hurt as much as it hurts right now. The good news is that it won't. Your anticipation of breakup hell is *actually* what breakup hell is. It's never going to be any worse than when you are anticipating how bad it could be.

Your job for today is to understand that you are in a temporary state. This will all end.

You will remember your ex and feel some kind of way, but there won't be a pang in your stomach. You will remember them without the emotional connection you have right now.

Journal: What is the worst thing that could happen? You feel like shit today, you feel like shit tomorrow. You can survive feeling like shit for a few days. Write about your fears of getting over this breakup. What are you really worried about?

a few reminders when you miss someone who didn't love you as much as you loved them:

"I've had it with all stingy-hearted sons of bitches. A heart is to be spent." —Stephen Dunn

"If you have to speculate if someone loves you and wants to be with you, chances are they don't. It's not that complicated. Love, in most cases, betrays the one feeling it. Don't waste moments waiting and wondering. Don't throw away your time dreaming of someone that doesn't want you. No one is that amazing, certainly not the one who would pass you up." —Donna Lynn Hope

"And you tried to change, didn't you? Closed your mouth more. Tried to be softer, prettier, less volatile, less awake….You can't make homes out of human beings. Someone should have already told you that. And if he wants to leave, then let him leave. You are terrifying, and strange, and beautiful. Something not everyone knows how to love." —Warsan Shire

"I miss your smile…but I miss mine more." —Laurel House

"To be rejected by someone doesn't mean you should also reject yourself or that you should think of yourself as a lesser person. It doesn't mean that nobody will ever love you anymore. Remember that only ONE person has rejected you at the moment, and it only hurt so much because to you, that person's opinion symbolized the opinion of the whole world, of God." —Jocelyn Soriano

"Had I not created my whole world, I would certainly have died in other people's." —Anais Nin

"You have to go through the fire. Avoiding the pain is why most people never resolve it. You have to dig deep, sit in it, and ugly cry." —Vanessa Williams

Journal: Write about one of these quotes that genuinely made you feel better and what was helpful about it for you to remember.

your ex probably wasn't that great, anyway

It's so easy to wear rose-colored glasses during your breakup and assume that you are missing out on the best relationship in the world simply because you have no choice in the matter. But your relationship was flawed; you know this because it ended. The other person was not enough for you, even if you were enough for them. Now you have to let it go.

Don't let yourself remember things being better than they actually were.

Refuse to mourn something you never got to enjoy in the first place.

When you remember your relationship and miss your ex, make sure you sprinkle in the *real* memories of just how dismissive or messy or indifferent they were. You owe it to yourself not to make your breakup any harder than it has to be. You do not have to mourn this perfect relationship you never had. You just have to let go of something temporary and flawed.

Journal: Make a long list of your ex's flaws. All the things they did that were mean-spirited or just annoyed you. Make sure the person you're hung up on is the real person you left behind.

read this every time
you doubt yourself

For today, read this:

"Why You'll Never Be Enough For Him" by Kim Quindlen

It's not that you're too heavy or too thin. It's not because you're too slutty or too much of a prude. It has nothing to do with the size of your breasts or your thighs or your stomach.

It's not that you're too successful or not successful enough. You could spend your entire life asking yourself what you did wrong or what it was about you that wasn't good enough for him, what it was that other women had that you were missing.

You'll never find the answer. Because there's nothing wrong with you. It's not that you aren't pretty enough or smart enough or confident enough. It's not your finances or your job or your friends.

You are just as you are supposed to be.
You are perfect even among
all of your imperfections.

As long as you maintain a thirst for life, a desire to work hard and live truthfully, and the willpower to grow and to improve yourself and to try harder every day, you are just as you should be.

You will never be enough for him because even the most perfect, flawless woman in the world—who does not exist—would never be enough for him.

It's him. He's part of a certain breed. A breed that does not want to accept you for who you are, because they're afraid of stopping the chase. They're afraid of settling down and trying to find the true kind of love, the kind in which your love for someone is so deep that you learn to accept them and to love them just as they are. The kind of love that is so deep that their beauty seems to radiate outwards from within.

This type of breed is afraid of stopping and trying to find that love. It's not necessarily the love that they're afraid of. It's the stopping. They're afraid of stopping and discovering that they will potentially never find that kind of love. They've rejected you because they're afraid of facing rejection themselves.

This type of breed does not apply to all men, just a small number. And it's just not with men that these fears of intimacy and rejection exist. There are women like this, too. There are people all over the world like this—people who continue to find issues in whomever they date, people who cannot accept anyone who's less than perfect. Because they know, subconsciously, that they will never find this person. The high standards, the no-one-is-good-enough mindset will keep them safe. It will keep them alone.

This is not meant to be an excuse. This is not to say that you are faultless. This is not to say that you have no responsibility in your relationships. You have to try, you have to compromise, you have to be vulnerable, and you have to put the other person in front of yourself. You have to work, you have to be selfless sometimes, you have to acknowledge that you have flaws, that you have made and will continue to make mistakes.

But sometimes, regardless of how hard you try, you find yourself desperately in love with someone who cannot love you back. Someone who refuses to accept you, because it's easier to make you think something's wrong with you than it is for them to be vulnerable and human and open to the idea of being hurt.

You cannot change them. You cannot fix them. You cannot fix you. Because you cannot apologize for who you are. You should not question what is wrong with you or what you're missing or what you need to change.

Someone who truly loves you, someone who is truly right for you, will not force you to turn inside yourself and search for what it is about you that is wrong, what it is that needs to be changed. A person who truly loves you will bring you outside of yourself. They will bring you out into the world. They will make you want more for yourself—more happiness, more knowledge, more adventure, more experiences. The list is endless. They will excite you and support you and inspire you to be better, instead of causing you to become trapped inside your own head, wondering how you can change yourself to make them happy.

When you've found real love, you'll know it. Because you'll always be enough, regardless of your flaws and your insecurities and your vulnerabilities. You will be enough for them anyways, and they will be enough for you.

Journal: No journaling assignment today. Read this as many times as you need to. Write if you want to.

"I must just be ugly/ overweight/unattractive."

This is how everyone feels after a relationship, and it's never true. Ugly/overweight/unattractive people find love all the time. If you think you could have kept your relationship by being more attractive, remember that the most beautiful people on the planet have all had their hearts broken by someone who didn't love them as much as they wanted.

If you think you need to lose weight in order to find love, you are wrong.

If you think you need to look more like an Instagram model to find love, you are wrong.

If you think you are too broken to find love, you are wrong.

If you think someone good won't pick you, you are wrong.

You do not need a better job to find love.

You do not need flawless skin to find love.

You don't need to have perfect eating habits to find love.

You do not need to cure your anxiety to find love.

You don't need to erase your past mistakes to find love.

You don't need to have a perfect relationship with your family to find love.

You are worthy of love right now.
You can find someone who loves you right now. There is no threshold of being a good or beautiful person you need to hit in order to be worthy of love.

When these thoughts appear, it's good to remind yourself that it's human nature to think this way. These thoughts will appear from time to time, but that doesn't mean they are true. They are just a car coming down the road; you can see it coming and you can observe it leaving. They are just errant anxiety thoughts; they aren't facts.

There are people out there who will love you just the way you are. The problem is you are focused on someone who did not (your ex). When you start to let your feelings for them go, you will open yourself up to the world of people who are ready to love and be loved by an imperfect human being just like you.

Journal: Explore any feelings you have about not feeling good enough to find love. Did any of these thoughts resonate with you? Talk about the barriers you think you have to finding someone who loves you, and then think about all the people with that quality that are happily in love.

no, it's not taking you "too long" to heal

There is no correct timeline for healing. It takes as long as it takes, and your job is just to keep putting one foot in front of the other.

It is easy to berate yourself for not moving on fast enough. It can feel like a race to be "over it" before your ex, even if you are the only one who will notice. The only race, the only winner, is going to be you when you are able to heal and move on as a better, wiser, stronger person.

When you get frustrated with yourself for not being over it yet, try to reframe this feeling as gratitude that you are getting all your feelings about the relationship out at once in this period of time so that one day soon you will be able to truly move on. Use and embrace this time; it is yours for a purpose. Instead of running away from your thoughts, you're going to embrace them and work through them and come out of this the best version of yourself.

Journal: Write about the gratitude you feel for how you are healing and how you have already healed.

when you're tired of trying to get over him

When you're doing the difficult work of dealing with a breakup, just getting up every day can lead to burnout. It's okay to want a break from all of this trying so hard. You deserve one.

The good news is that so much of getting over a breakup is just getting through the day. When you can't muster up the energy to be an active participant in your life, you can trust that time and distance are still working their powerful magic.

Zone out for a day with a page-turner mystery book or a good series on Netflix. Remind yourself that all you have to do today is just make it until the end. It will be easier tomorrow.

Journal: Make a list of 10 things you're grateful for. Think about all the little things that can hold you over until the day is through and you wake up one day more numb to their memory.

it's not your job to punish your ex

It sucks when someone hurts you and they don't get punished. It can be easy to become obsessed with watching someone like this from afar, waiting for them to get their comeuppance. We all have an innate desire to dispense justice, but this is counterproductive.

The more energy you spend wanting to get revenge on your ex, the more energy you put into a relationship that is already dead. You are pouring water through a sieve. There is no end result that will feel satisfying to you. Your ex, whether or not they are dealt justice, is no longer any of your business.

Today you are going to take the best care of yourself that you can, which means you are going to trash the idea that it is important for you to punish your ex. You get to move on and walk away from any perceived responsibilities you *think* you have toward them.

Wash your hands;
your ex is someone else's responsibility now.

Journal: Write about how it would feel to get revenge on your ex. Then write about how it would feel to really give up on getting even with them. Think about how each scenario makes you feel.

you're allowed to grieve

It doesn't matter how long you dated them. It doesn't matter if you were girlfriend-boyfriend official or if you were a side chick. You loved someone, you opened yourself up, and your efforts weren't reciprocated. You're allowed to be hurt. You are allowed to grieve.

Be suspicious of anyone who tries to make you feel guilty for being hurt.

The only way to get rid of a feeling is to feel the feeling. If you're embarrassed and try to hide or deny a feeling, it's just going to take a lot longer to let go of it.

You had vulnerable moments with this person. You hoped for more vulnerable moments in the future. In the olden days a guy would see a woman from a distance and start writing love letters. You traded bodily fluids and developed oxytocin as a result of this person. Please don't let anyone make you feel weird about missing them.

Journal: Write about how you miss your ex. It's okay to admit out loud (or on paper) the extent of the feelings to which you are saying goodbye. It might even make sense how much you hurt when you realize that you're giving up a really beautiful future you dreamed up.

things that will make you feel better if you really think you're going to die alone:

—There's no accounting for a whirlwind romance. You could meet someone tomorrow and be seriously falling for them a week from now. It only takes one person.

—People fall in love at different times in their life. You don't have to fall in love by the time you are 24 or 30 or 49. And if you think about it, you are already in the most exciting part of your life *now* while you're dating and the promise of love is perpetually around the corner.

—The time you spend being single and working on yourself will pay dividends for the rest of your life. While you're not spending your time and energy on another person, you spend it on yourself. Your future career, health, self-esteem, and life accomplishments will thank you for this time. You'll probably also have closer friendships, and when you *do* get in a relationship it will likely be a lot healthier emotionally than if you'd just been in one your entire adult life.

—You can be lonely in a relationship. It's a lot easier to deal with being lonely as a single person.

—Being single means you have one leg up on everyone who is in a crappy relationship. At least you don't still have to break up with someone and *then* start where you are now. It can take months and years to separate yourself from someone physically, financially, and legally.

— Your friends in relationships are posting their best moments on social media. They aren't posting about their fights or the way their partner doesn't live up to what they dreamed a husband or wife would be like. Scroll through your own social media and think about the impression someone would get from the outside vs. what you've really gone through. Apply this perspective to anyone's life that makes you feel insecure.

— You won't always have the opportunity you have right now: to make your life 100% the way you want it without having to take anyone else's opinion into account.

—It's normal to feel the way you feel.

—Now that you have perspective and can see how flawed they are, would you have *really* wanted to end up with any of your exes?

—Beyoncé was single once, too.

Journal: Write about one of these refrains that genuinely made you feel better and what is helpful about it for you to remember.

fuck yes or fuck no

The way to stop overanalyzing your relationships is to understand that loving behavior typically doesn't need to be analyzed.

Writer Mark Manson (author of *The Subtle Art of Not Giving a F*ck*) has a well-loved essay called *Fuck Yes or No* in which he argues that if you need to overanalyze someone's behavior, they probably just aren't right for you. Someone who loves you won't leave you wondering whether they love you. They'll want the best for you. They'll fight for you.

When someone likes you but doesn't love you, they'll make excuses and you'll make excuses for them. This is bad. Mark calls this "the law of fuck yes or no":

> *"The Law of 'Fuck Yes or No' states that when you want to get involved with someone new, in whatever capacity, they must inspire you to say 'Fuck Yes' in order for you to proceed with them.*
>
> *The Law of 'Fuck Yes or No' also states that when you want to get involved with someone new, in whatever capacity, THEY must respond with a 'Fuck Yes' in order for you to proceed with them."*

It seems like this law is going to ask you to give up a lot, but all you have to do is give up on people who are lukewarm about you. Getting rid of them is a gift.

Journal: You can find the whole essay published online on Mark's website; directions are in the Recommended Reading section at the end of this book. Find and read the piece and then journal about what feelings it inspires in you.

you are losing so much less than you thought you were

All those times when you get sad missing your former love, make sure you challenge the narrative that's in your head. Most of the time you are mourning something you never had. You are thinking about the future you wanted with this person where they showered you with love and you'd worked out all your problems and magically gotten on the same page about everything.

You never had that future to grieve. It is not, and never has been, real.

This may sound like tough love, but it really isn't. There is a huge switch that's going to flick inside you when you understand that you are losing so much less than you thought you were.

You didn't lose what you think you lost. All the good and amazing things you brought to the relationship are still there. They are present inside you, and you will have them with the next one. You lost someone who was halfhearted enough about you to let you go. You didn't lose that much.

Journal: Write about what you're feeling today, wherever you are. Just check in and free write; you'll be able to see what you're feeling and what you need right now.

just because you're single doesn't mean you're alone

When you're single you will want to wallow in your loneliness. You can do that. It might feel cathartic to cry and explore this thing so many people are afraid of—the state of being alone.

But you must understand in your bones that being lonely has nothing to do with being alone. You can be lonely with another person, or you can be lonely by yourself—and it's a whole lot easier to fix yourself than it is to fix a relationship. Your marital status is irrelevant; loneliness hits everyone from time to time.

The way to deal with being lonely is to figure out what makes you feel satisfied in life and connected to people, and to spend some time doing that. Take a community education class, go on a yoga retreat, call up a friend or family member and have a long chat, write a nice email or text message to someone, join a Facebook or Reddit community for a niche interest you have, try Bumble BFF or Meetup, foster a dog or cat, work from a coffee shop instead of home, organize a happy hour or party, volunteer, or walk or run in a public park during a busy time of day. Even something like getting your hair cut and having someone else touch you affectionately while they are washing your hair can feel so healthy.

Journal: Make a list of things that would make your life feel more "full" and less lonely. Try one of them.

your issues live in your tissues

Physical movement can help you heal. Getting outside and taking long walks will help you relax and work through your feelings. Getting a massage will be cathartic. Doing a "Yoga with Adriene" video on YouTube will help you reconnect with yourself and feel good about the way you are helping yourself heal from your breakup.

This is not the same as going to the gym to try to get a "revenge body" where all your focus is still placed on your ex and how they might perceive you. It's also not about pressuring yourself to fit into a mold.

You're not trying to change yourself; you're trying to *become* yourself.

Find ways to stimulate your body that feel good to you. Don't push yourself to take up running or do something that doesn't feel natural. Lean into what is already there. Maybe you love swimming but it's no longer summer—find an indoor pool you can use. Go on a walking date with a friend to catch up on gossip while you stretch your legs. Walk somewhere instead of driving.

Journal: Document how movement made you feel.

you don't need a relationship to be happy

There are people who are happy and joyful who are also single, even people who are reluctantly single but still thriving.

You need to let go of the idea that the only way for you to be happy is to be in the relationship you are picturing in your head for your future. You are smart and tenacious. No matter what hand life deals to you, you will find a way to be happy.

This is your life, and you should start living it now—not when you've locked down Mr. or Ms. Right. Work on making your life look as much like you dreamed of when you were a kid as possible. Maybe now is the time to move to a new city or change careers. Maybe it's time to go out on a limb and join a dance team or try out for your church choir.

Whatever makes you happy is what you should embrace during this period.

Journal: Make a pie chart of things that make you happy. Identify which of those pie pieces you have control over (or if there's anything missing that you would like to be included). Spend time this week working to increase those things so that your pie chart is full of healthy, fulfilling activities that add up to a satisfying life.

pie chart here
↓

you can't let one person ruin your life (a pep talk)

Your life is so much bigger than this person you lost.

They are one person. They aren't important enough to ruin your life. You aren't going to let them be that important.

No matter what they do, they are always just one person, and you are always so much stronger than them. You can pull yourself through this because no matter what happens, you always still have yourself.

Think about yourself as a teammate. You are the strongest, smartest, most tenacious person you could ask for. You are wise, and you know what your needs are right now.

Please don't dishonor yourself by thinking that this person was the best you could do. You will fall in love again (and again, and again, if you want to). You will meet new people in new cities and have moments in your life where you will laugh at how silly you were for grieving this one person when there was so much waiting for you.

This is a painful experience; it's not your one and only shot at love.

Journal: Write about your dreams for the future. Let yourself get excited knowing that you can take yourself anywhere.

gratitude as a grounding technique

When things seem to be spinning out of control, you can use your gratitude practice as a grounding technique.

Make a list of 10 things you're thankful for. If that's daunting, pick three. Look at your list and breathe. Remind yourself that no matter what happens, you will always have things to be thankful for. It's likely that many of the things you included on your list aren't going anywhere. Life is bigger than this person who left you.

The fact that a small part of your life is changing doesn't negate all these other things for which you are thankful.

Keeping a gratitude practice helps you when you are feeling most lost, alone, and worried about the future. It is a foundation that reminds you of all the ways you are blessed and all the reasons you have to look forward to tomorrow. If you're freaked out in the moment, take three deep breaths and with each breath, try to name something you are thankful for. You could try doing this each time you wash your hands or go to the bathroom. Throughout the day, you will ground yourself to what's working in your life.

Journal: Make your gratitude list.

pain has to be felt before it can leave

The reason your pain is still lingering is because you haven't felt all of it yet. The only way to get rid of pain in your life is to feel it. This takes time and vulnerability and the ability to slowly move through it.

You can't force your way through, and unfortunately it's not a speedy trip.

Your journaling process helps you get pain out every day. Every day you are getting closer to not having to feel these feelings about your ex. Every time you cry, you are getting closer to moving on.

Try watching sad movies or sad TV shows (hello, *This Is Us*). Having emotional experiences, even ones unrelated to your relationship, will help you cycle through all the emotions stuck inside you and get them out. When you are frustrated about the time it takes to get over someone, you can relax with the knowledge that it will happen naturally and all by itself. All you have to do is continue being open and rather than avoiding your emotions, work through them as they arise.

Journal: What pain are you still holding onto? Is there anything you are afraid to work through?

this is your turning point

Everyone on earth tries to avoid something bad happening to them, and yet in retrospect everyone always says that the bad thing that happened was a gift.

JK Rowling famously began writing the *Harry Potter* series when she was broke, newly divorced, and on public assistance. Because the life she knew had disintegrated around her, it was the perfect foundation for her to build something new.

It's cheesy, but every end is the beginning of something else.

Grieve what you lost, but don't feel that things are hopeless or like your whole life is bad. It's not up for debate: In the future you *will* look back on this as the beginning of a positive step in your life. You're not going to look back and still regret losing your relationship; no one does that. It doesn't happen. Repeat to yourself and believe that this is an exciting new period in your life. When you feel like saying, "It's over," instead say, "It's beginning." The best things in your life are going to happen now that you are free to pursue them. It's a fresh start and you can use it for whatever you want.

Journal: Write about your wildest hopes for what this new life period is going to be like.

treasure your time out

After a breakup, you get to take some time alone to heal and figure out what you want to do next.

Try to consistently bring your attention back to the knowledge that this is a period in which all you have to do is rest. You get to indulge yourself and catch up on sleep. Eat food you are genuinely craving. Read and watch content that feels good to you. Focus on little pleasures that make your body and mind feel happy.

When things seem hard, remember that there is no pressure to do anything or behave a certain way. All you have to do right now is take care of yourself. You get to buckle down and focus on something simple.

This is a good mantra to adopt for a while if you're someone who struggles with self-care and feel like you can't indulge in it because it's "selfish":

"All you have to do right now is take care of yourself."

Journal: Write about what it would mean for you to be someone who is attentively taking care of your own needs right now.

gentleness is the move

A good way to make your life 1,000% better is to embrace gentleness.

When your friend is late to meet you for dinner, think about how their life is busy and how it happens to everyone and how you'd rather be a generous person who can forgive than spend the next 10 minutes being crabby at someone you love. When you're working out and you see someone's spandex hugging them in an unflattering way, think of a compliment about that person and repeat it in your head. Smile and say something nice to a random person in the coffee shop line.

Doing these things may be hard. You're probably exhausted. You're probably thinking that it's supposed to be your turn to be doted on.

But a strange thing will start to happen if you approach other people with gentleness. Those gentle thoughts are going to turn inward. You measure yourself with the same stick you measure other people with. If you're gentle with others, you will be gentle with yourself. And right now, you need gentleness.

Journal: Write a few gentle thoughts about someone who is annoying you right now. Practice being generous and gracious and treating that person like a kindly, wise, rich grandmother who can see the mistakes other people are making but is too joyful and rich and well-cared for to be put out by them.

your feelings are valid

No one else can tell you how to feel. No one has the authority to tell you that what you are feeling is wrong. If you feel it, it's the correct thing to feel.

Life is a funny winding road and sometimes things hurt more or less than they are "supposed" to. Something might hit us particularly hard because we're at a vulnerable place in life or just because it reminds us of previous rejections. Or perhaps you have really solid footing in life right now and you're feeling better than you think is appropriate.

Whatever you are feeling is exactly what you are supposed to be feeling.

Allow it. Lean into it. Be the student to your mind's teacher. Don't let yourself feel guilty for whatever reaction you are having.

Journal: Take note of any shadowy feelings that are lingering—anything you are avoiding. Write about it.

it's okay to miss them

Don't let anyone make you feel inferior for missing your ex. You're allowed to miss them. You're allowed to admit that your life together had good moments. You're allowed to feel sad.

While it's important not to dwell on the happy memories you have from your relationship, it's also important not to ignore them. You have to know what you are giving up in order to move on.

Don't let yourself pretend you were never happy with your ex.

If you catch yourself missing them, you miss them. It's just the reality of the situation. Ignoring this won't help you move on. Let yourself feel comfortable with the truth. You're not doing anything wrong. Any normal, loving human would miss someone if they were in the same situation you find yourself in.

Journal: Write about a happy memory you have with your ex and how you hope to incorporate whatever created that moment into your next relationship.

what to do if you don't have closure

The unfortunate truth about not having closure is that you're just going to have to get over it anyway.

Closure helps; it tells you a nice story that can be the first paved rocks in the path to getting over him or her—but it isn't necessary.

People get dumped without closure all the time. It isn't pleasant and it isn't respectful. But it happens. And those people get over their ex, too.

Your ex's refusal to give you closure is itself a kind of closure. They are showing you the kind of person they are. They are willing to dishonor the good times and intimate moments you've had together in order to spare themselves from an uncomfortable conversation. This is a nice springboard into wanting to get the fuck away from them and everything they stand for.

Sometimes you just don't get closure. It really sucks. But you have to move on. You have to repeat to yourself that this person cared so little for you that they don't *want* you to know what really happened. They are terrified that you will know the truth—which is that the whole relationship hinged on them growing up and being a decent person, and that never happened.

A lack of closure *is* closure. The closure is that they are a shitty, immature person and your life is better without them. Focus on the future and on to the next one.

Journal: Write your own closure. Tell yourself the story of why they ended it. Go ahead and assume the worst about them; it will make for a cohesive story.

breaking down doesn't mean you are broken

Don't get down on yourself about your relationship ending. This is something that truly does happen to everyone and has nothing to do with your value or worth as a dating partner. You will get over them. This might be a period where you feel bad, but it's not a period that is going to break you.

Humans are amazing creatures who adapt to multitudes of unpleasant circumstances very quickly. If we are good at anything, we are good at surviving. When you feel weak because you are missing your ex or having a nostalgic, emotional day, know that you will exit this whole experience as a stronger person.

As bad as it gets, it's never going to be the end of your life.

There will always be somewhere you can go. There will always be people you can turn to. There will always be something new to hope for.

Journal: Write about how strong and resilient you are. Thank yourself for how supportive you are being to your needs right now. Name specific ways you are doing a good job at taking care of yourself.

reminders to build your confidence after experiencing rejection:

—Breakups happen to everyone. Every type of person experiences rejection.

—Your breakup isn't a rejection of you, it's a statement about who your partner was and where they were in their life. Not fitting with ONE person on the planet doesn't say anything about your worth.

—Just because ONE person rejects you doesn't mean there aren't many other people who would love to be with you. Your breakup does not give you this information.

—You don't want to be a generic person who fits with everyone. You want to fit with the person who really matters.

—The most successful people also get rejected the most often. They are out on a limb *fighting* for what they want. If you are fighting to be in love and in the happiest, healthiest relationship possible, you are going to find a lot of people you don't fit with along the way. This means a lot of rejection.

—But again, this rejection is not a rejection of you, it's a rejection of how you fit with this other person.

—Each rejection teaches you how to be better.

—Only people who truly live life scared as hell of anything that's beyond their control live life without being rejected. This is a VERY sad life that you do not want to emulate.

—Each rejection means you tried—that you did the one and only thing you are supposed to do in this life, which is to go out and try to get something that matters to you. Congratulations on living.

Journal: For this one journal entry, force yourself to be positive. Write about the good things that have come from this breakup, or about nice things you like about yourself, or about what you are excited for in the future. Make today about feeling good about yourself.

the world is full of opportunities for you to love and be loved

The most freeing realization you will have during your breakup is that the One who left you is not the only One. Every day is a new opportunity to meet someone you may fall in love with. The world is full of potential suitors.

I know a common understanding nowadays is that people suck and that good people are rare, but I reject that scarcity mentality and you can, too.

How many good people are you friends with? How many people have you come alive while talking to without realizing their potential beforehand? If you've ever fallen more in love with someone the longer you knew them, you already know this truth: When you look with hopeful eyes, there are so many good people around who can take this journey with you.

Think about your close friends—would you pick them off a single photo on a dating app? If you'd date them in real life but you wouldn't pick them from afar, you know that you have some work to do opening up who you think might be a match.

Instead of seeing life as a waiting game where you are uncomfortable and on edge until you find your forever person, consider that your life could be full of love affairs. You could fall in love with so many people and have so many incredible experiences before you meet your forever person. Which of these scenarios sounds more fun?

Journal: Reflect on the people you know in real life that make high-quality partners. Write about whether you would give them a chance if you saw them on an app not knowing anything about them.

your ex has already served their purpose

One way to move on from an ex is to focus on the ways they have already fulfilled their purpose for being in your life. They were here to teach you a lesson. They don't need to stick around after the lesson is done. Their purpose now is to move aside and make room for the next person.

The real push here is to reframe your thoughts of someone leaving you as thoughts about how they have completed their time with you. Like a piece of plastic that once kept a delicious candy bar safe and sanitary, you have enjoyed the candy bar; why would you hang onto the wrapper?

This approach emphasizes that you have no unfinished business with your ex. There is no reason to reach out to them or to miss them.

You'll keep yourself focused ahead, looking at what is coming next.

Journal: Write about the things that really do feel "complete" now that your relationship has ended. What purpose do you think they served in your life?

you're supposed to practice loving like it's yoga

One of the most powerful love lessons I ever learned was from Tracy McMillan, who during an interview with Oprah told me that I'm supposed to practice loving like it's yoga.

This idea is so freeing because daily yoga truly is a *practice*. It's something you work at and get different perspectives about and check in with yourself about—but it's not a competition. You aren't supposed to have yoga *perfection*; you're supposed to have a yoga *practice*. The expectation is that you have a lifetime of lessons ahead of you.

It's the same way with love. Love is something you practice and work at every day. You love imperfectly and you do the best you can. There's no expectation of being good at it off the bat and never having to think about it again. You know it's something you're going to work on forever.

You have the rest of your life to learn and improve at giving and receiving love. You don't have to be perfect at it today.

Journal: What would it mean for you to "practice" being good at love?

ways to interrupt
unproductive anxiety

Even if you're not an anxious person, a lot of people experience anxiety as a result of their breakup. Going forward, you'll want to create some catchall grounding thoughts you can return to when things are getting rough inside your head. Here are some thoughts you can challenge yourself with when you notice yourself experiencing anxiety:

—You have a success rate of 100% at getting yourself through difficult situations. You will get through this one, too.

—The rule of five: If it's not going to matter in five years, don't spend more than five minutes worrying about it.

—Someone has survived worse. No matter who you are and what your situation is, someone else has been there, survived, and made their life better on the other side.

—Feelings aren't facts. Your anxiety brain is like someone on Facebook posting fake news memes. Just because you see them doesn't mean you have to believe them.

—What if the problem you are worrying about only exists because you are trying to solve it? What would it look like to spend your energy accepting the situation instead of trying to change it?

—This Buddha quote: "You can only lose what you cling to."

—Every challenge you've already conquered in your life looked just as scary at some point.

—Try to think this way: "I can't control the situation, but I can unplug and practice breathing. I know I will feel better if I take a break and exercise or listen to music or do yoga, so I choose to do that."

Journal: Write some calming thoughts for you to ground yourself with when your breakup anxiety creeps up.

you should forgive them

Forgiveness is for the person doing the forgiving, not the person being forgiven.

When you forgive your ex for any misdeeds they did while you were together, you aren't doing it because they deserve your forgiveness. Whether they deserve your forgiveness is irrelevant. You are going to forgive them because *you* deserve to move on, and you can't move on when you are busy hating someone.

Forgiving someone is a selfish act.

When you forgive someone you are releasing the psychic hold they have on you. You are saying that you no longer want to offer this person a rent-free space in your brain where you will think about how much you hate them. Forgiveness is the opposite of being stuck in love with someone. Forgiveness is letting them go and moving on.

Journal: Write a letter of forgiveness to your ex. You won't send it to them, so be as sappy as you want to be. Forgive them for everything they did wrong in the relationship—not because they deserve it, but because you do. [Use a separate piece of paper for this letter].

Chrissy Stockton is a writer, thinker, and creative cheerleader based on the internet. She has a degree in philosophy and if she could have any superpower, she would be able to talk to dogs. Chrissy is the author of *We Are All Just A Collection Of Cords*, a poetry collection, and creator of the essay compilation *What I Didn't Post On Instagram*. Follow her on Instagram @x.lane.s.

Recommended Websites / Podcasts:

bit.ly/difficult-truths-about-love

bit.ly/why-youll-never-be-enough-for-him

markmanson.net/fuck-yes

bit.ly/let-go-bananas

Tracy McMillan on Oprah's SuperSoul podcast

Recommended Books

101 Essays That Will Change The Way You Think
—*Brianna Wiest*

We Are All Just A Collection of Cords
—*Chrissy Stockton*

Salt Water
—*Brianna Wiest*

It'll Be Okay, And You Will Be Too.
—*Jeremy Goldberg*

THOUGHT
CATALOG
Books

THOUGHTCATALOG.COM
NEW YORK · LOS ANGELES